INTRODUCTION

In 1988, the DHSS Committee on Medical Aspects of Food Policy published *Present day practice in infant feeding: Third report.*[1] The report reviews the latest scientific information about infant feeding and draws on the results of three national surveys of infant feeding practices, carried out in 1975, 1980 and 1985 among mothers in all socio-economic groups.[2]

This booklet is based on those reports and sets out the information most relevant to those who advise parents about feeding their babies and young children. It is not intended to supply information about particular products or individual circumstances.

1

BREASTFEEDING

HEALTH VALUE

Breastfeeding provides the best nutrition for healthy infants. The milk from a healthy mother who is taking a varied, balanced diet is a complete and unique food which is of particular value in the early months and can contribute an important part of the mixed diet in later infancy.

Successful breastfeeding enables the mother and infant to feel close together and to get to know each other while providing a convenient and hygienic way of feeding. Human milk is a living material with enzymes which assist digestion, and antibodies and active cells which contribute to the body's defences against infection.

Colostrum provides all the nutrients and fluid that the newborn baby needs. The composition of the mature milk which comes later is adapted specifically to promote optimal growth and to lessen the risks from allergy and infection. The absorption of the nutrients in human milk from the baby's gut is generally very efficient.

There are considerable variations in the composition of the milk from one mother to another and from time to time in the milk of the same woman. However, fat and milk sugar (lactose) are always the most important sources of energy. The protein fraction consists mainly of whey proteins, some of which serve a primarily anti-infective rather than a nutritive function.

ENCOURAGING SUCCESSFUL BREASTFEEDING

Successful breastfeeding is facilitated by:

☐ Putting the baby to the mother's breast very soon after birth

☐ Correct positioning at the breast

☐ Feeding on demand rather than at set times

☐ Not giving complementary feeds

☐ A positive and relaxed atmosphere, and

☐ Supportive and consistent advice.

Samples of infant formula should not be given to mothers.

There should be good liaison and continuity of advice and support when the mother leaves hospital. This is particularly important now that most mothers have been discharged before breastfeeding is fully established.

Successful breastfeeding needs to be encouraged by ensuring that mothers are free to feed their babies when and where they need to. This may involve changes in society's attitudes to breastfeeding mothers and, at a more practical level, the provision of baby care facilities such as those being promoted under the National Baby Care Symbol (shown opposite).

National Baby Care symbol

BOTTLE FEEDING

NUTRITIONAL VALUE

Infant formulas are manufactured products which, when used according to instructions, provide a nutritionally complete food for young infants. However, unlike human milk, infant formulas contain no living cells, active enzymes or human anti-infective factors. Infant formulas are suitable throughout the first year and may be used as part of the weaning diet.

Most infant formulas are based on cow milk, and either caseins or whey proteins predominate. Those formulas with a dominance of whey have been manufactured to produce an amino-acid pattern more like that of human milk. The common practice of changing from a whey dominant to a casein dominant formula as the baby gets older has not been proven to be beneficial.

Infant formulas of entirely vegetable origin have soya protein isolate as the main source of protein. These may be used in most cases when an alternative to an infant formula based on cow milk is required.

Vitamins and some minerals are added to infant formulas during manufacture to allow for losses during processing and storage. Other adjustments are made to offset the less efficient absorption of some nutrients from infant formulas by the gut.

The nutrient composition of infant formulas is regulated by official guidelines and international standards. Marketing should comply with the principles of the WHO code as reflected by the voluntary code of practice drawn up between the Government and the Food Manufacturers' Federation (now the Food and Drink Federation).

ADVICE TO MOTHERS

Errors in the making up of feeds and poor hygiene practices are most hazardous for babies under the age of 6 months.

☐ Mothers should be shown how to make up a bottle feed.

☐ They need advice about how to avoid microbial contamination by using sterilising chemicals or boiling the bottles and teats.

☐ Heating in a microwave oven does not ensure sterility of the bottles and there is the risk of scalds if feeds are heated in this way.

WEANING

During weaning, the exclusively milk-fed infant becomes accustomed to a diet which contains all or most of the foods eaten by the rest of the family.

STARTING SOLID FOOD

Babies vary greatly in how quickly or easily they take to solids and experiment with foods of different consistency, texture, flavour and colour. The guidelines given below depend on developmental factors as well as on nutritional considerations. It is unwise to introduce solids too early, before the baby has developed more mature mucosal and systemic defence mechanisms against infection and allergy. Lumpier foods should not be given until a baby is ready to bite and chew. On the other hand, if solids are introduced too late, undernutrition and feeding difficulties may arise.

Some infants are offered a diet which omits nutritionally important foods. Their families may be strongly influenced by cultural or religious beliefs, or they may be misapplying current information about diet and nutrition. Expert advice is sometimes needed to ensure that the diet remains adequate.

When infants are weaned on to a vegetarian diet, it is important to consider whether the diet is adequate in respect of energy, protein and iron.

The following general guidelines are recommended:

☐ Very young babies do not need food other than milk. It is best to wait until the baby is at least 3 months old before introducing solids.

☐ By 6 months, most babies will have needed to take an expanded diet.

☐ By the age of 9 or 10 months, babies can be given a wide range of home-made and commercial food. A varied diet is more likely to provide all the nutrients needed for normal growth and health during infancy and childhood.

☐ To avoid hypernatraemia, weaning foods should not contain excessive amounts of salt.

MILK

Milk is an important source of energy, calcium, riboflavin and vitamin A for pre-school children.

Human milk and infant formula are the only milks which should be given in the first 5-6 months and they can be continued with advantage up to 1 year.

From 6 months, whole pasteurised cow milk, which is cheap, convenient and nutritious, may be given. Follow-up milk may also be used and it is a good source of iron. Skimmed milk is not recommended for infants and children under the age of 5 years.

Soya-based milks may be used for infants who appear to be intolerant of cow milk, but only those called infant formula are nutritionally adequate. Goat milk may be used for babies over 6 months, as long as it is pasteurised.

THE TODDLER'S DIET

EATING FOR HEALTH

Many parents are concerned that their children should develop healthy patterns of eating from an early age. This is sensible provided that the diet meets the child's current nutritional needs.

Many families have cut down on whole milk, full fat dairy products, fatty meats, fried foods and sugars. They now eat more low fat dairy foods (including skimmed milk), foods high in polyunsaturates and fibre-rich foods such as wholemeal bread, cereals, vegetables, salads and fruit.

Normal growth and activity are good indicators of whether a toddler's diet is adequate. With toddlers, it is important to remember that a diet of bulky foods with low calorie content (low energy density) may not supply sufficient energy. Many fibre-rich foods impair absorption of some important nutrients such as calcium and iron and should be offered only in moderation.

The following advice is recommended:

☐ Full fat milk is preferred for children below 5 years. Semi-skimmed milk and dairy products, but not skimmed milk, may be progressively introduced from the age of 24 months, provided the overall diet is adequate.

☐ The misuse of sugary foods should be avoided because they may lead to dental caries.

☐ Fresh fruit and raw vegetables make good snacks.

☐ The toddler's diet should not be over-salted, and it is wise not to add salt at the table.

DIET AND CARDIOVASCULAR DISEASE

For adults, the COMA Report[3] on diet and cardiovascular disease made the following recommendations:

✱ No more than 35% of food energy should be derived from fat.

✱ No more than 15% of food energy should be from saturated fatty acids.

✱ Fibre-rich foods containing complex fibre-rich carbohydrates are preferred to simple sugars.

✱ Excessive intake of common salt should be avoided.

SPECIAL DIETARY CONSIDERATIONS

FAILURE TO THRIVE

If an infant fails to thrive, there may be an obvious cause which is easy to correct, such as underfeeding. If simple steps do not bring a rapid improvement, full medical and social investigations must be made.

VITAMINS

The newborn is usually well supplied with vitamins.

There may be vitamin deficiency:

— if the mother had an inadequate diet before and during pregnancy, or

— if the baby was born pre-term.

In the first 6 months, there is an adequate supply of vitamins, provided that:

— the infant is breastfed and the mother is getting an adequate diet; or

— the infant is given infant formula.
Infants who are considered to be at risk may be given supplementary vitamin drops from 1 month of age.

From 6 months on, the infant's vitamin stores may be depleted. The following advice is recommended to guard against deficiency:

■ A varied diet with some fortified foods should be encouraged.

■ Infants and young children need some sunlight as it is the main natural source of Vitamin D.

■ Supplementary vitamin drops are recommended for all children from 6 months to 5 years.

IRON

Iron deficiency in infants and toddlers occurs:

— if the iron stores are low, for example in babies born pre-term; or

— if there is insufficient iron in the diet, or if it is in a form which is not easily absorbed.

To prevent iron deficiency, the following guidelines are recommended:

■ The diet should contain some meat, poultry or fish.

■ An ample vitamin C intake is of particular importance for infants who are not eating meat or fish, as it enhances the relatively poor absorption of iron from vegetable sources.

■ The consumption of some iron fortified foods is encouraged.

FOOD INTOLERANCE

Some food intolerance is due to allergy which implies a disorder of the immune system. Eczema, wheezing and gastro-intestinal problems are examples of disorders which have been attributed to food allergy. Several foods and items in the diet have been suggested as causes. Children who have a family history of allergic disorders (atopy) have a greater risk of allergy themselves, but the type and severity of the allergic symptoms in an individual child depend on both genetic and environmental influences.

The following advice may be beneficial:

For potentially allergic children from atopic families:

■ Breastfeeding should be encouraged and care taken to avoid the early introduction of any other foods.

■ A soya-based infant formula may be used instead of one based on cow milk, but these formulas may also be allergenic.

■ From 6 months, infant formula or follow-up milk may be less allergenic than fresh cow milk.

■ It is wise to delay the introduction of fresh cow milk, eggs, wheat, nuts and citrus fruits. These foods should first be given in small amounts.

For infants with suspected food allergy:

■ The suspected food may be withdrawn for a short trial period. Prolonged dietary change (for example cutting out all milk) requires expert advice.

There are other types of food intolerance. Some infants cannot digest or absorb particular components of the diet. For example, some infants are intolerant of lactose due to lack of the enzyme lactase; impaired absorption induced by gluten occurs in coeliac disease. Other children suffer from rare metabolic disorders such as phenylketonuria or galactosaemia. Such children all need special diets carefully supervised by a dietitian.

Toddlers often go through a phase of refusing food or showing preferences for certain foods. Some develop strong dislikes (food aversion) which may last a long time. These behaviours are not usually due to true food intolerance.

DENTAL HEALTH

In general, children have less dental decay than before, but rampant caries still occurs. Three safeguards for dental health are important:

■ Promotion of good general health and oral hygiene.

■ Adequate but not excessive exposure to fluoride by the use of fluoride-containing toothpaste and an intake of fluoride from the water supply or from supplementary drops.

■ Avoiding too many sugary foods, especially between meals, as this may lead to dental caries.

WATER

A safe water supply is a prime requirement in infant nutrition. Every effort should be made to use water that is safe from water-borne infections and contaminants.

To minimise the danger of infection, the following advice is recommended:

■ For babies under 6 months, all water for making up feeds or for giving to infants, including bottled water, should be boiled.

■ Infants over 6 months can be given water freshly drawn from the public supply, without boiling.

Public water supplies deliver water of satisfactory quality. However, under certain conditions, in times of drought for example, the concentration of nitrate or of sodium may rise to undesirable levels in which case the Medical Officer for Environmental Health is notified so that necessary action may be taken.

If a private water supply is used or if water is drawn from a well, it is wise to ask the local authority whether the water is suitable for infants.

In houses with lead plumbing, the tap water may not always be suitable for making up feeds. Parents may need advice about the practical steps they can take, suitable to their local circumstances, to reduce any risk.

Water treated with a salt regenerated ion exchange softener is not suitable for regularly making up infant feeds because of the high sodium content.

EDUCATION ABOUT INFANT FEEDING

NATIONAL SURVEY 1985[2]

In 1985, 64% of mothers in Britain breastfed their babies at birth. The highest rate, 74%, was in London and the South East. The rate fell progressively from the South to the North of England, and the lowest rate of 48% was in Scotland. Young mothers and mothers in social classes IV and V were the groups with the lowest rates of breastfeeding.

By the sixth week only 39% of mothers were breastfeeding their babies. The most common reasons for giving up breastfeeding were said to be insufficient milk and sore nipples.

Of the bottlefed newborn babies, about 80% were started on whey dominant infant formulas. Use of casein dominant formulas increased with age so that at 4-5 months, more than half the bottlefed babies were given this type of formula.

The results of the 1985 survey show a slight trend towards a decline in breastfeeding when compared with the similar survey carried out in 1980.

In 1985, 30% of first time mothers said that they had decided how to feed their babies before they became pregnant. In later pregnancies, even more had come to a firm decision. In the same year, 10% of primigravidas had no antenatal discussion about infant feeding.

If the rates of breastfeeding are to be increased, it is important to influence the opinion of society as a whole. Health professionals should use every opportunity to influence the teaching of children and young people.

Parents should be given sufficient information and opportunity for discussion so that they can make an informed choice.

Once a mother has decided how she plans to feed her baby, health professionals should help her to succeed and there are voluntary groups which help to provide this support (National Childbirth Trust, Association of Breastfeeding Mothers, La Leche League). Breastfeeding mothers value the advice of professionals, especially when lactation begins.

It is worthwhile for all mothers to learn how to prepare an infant formula feed, but it is important to ensure that nothing detracts from the message about the desirability of breastfeeding.

Books, leaflets, videos and Open University courses are available, and some of them are free. However, these materials should be used only as a supplement to personal care from informed and sympathetic health professionals and lay support groups.